CARDS IN THE MIRROR

ARMANDO DE ARMAS

CARDS IN THE MIRROR

The Book That Anticipated The Appearance Of The Q Movement A Year Before

Foreword by Emilio Ichikawa

Translation by Frank Rodríguez
Style Revision by Armando De-Armas III

EXODUS

Summary

Truth and Sympathies in the U.S. Political Parties

CARDS IN THE MIRROR, by Armando de Armas, is a paradoxical attempt to make some things clear, but the way to the light doesn't always consist of leaving signals along the way as much as knocking down those already in place. It profanes concepts and beliefs with which we will certainly feel uncomfortable.

This essay has had the purpose and the occasion to appear in the context of the 2012 U.S. electoral contest. In that context it evokes history and demarcates concepts of interest to the main parties in contention. In this circumstance, however, rather than influencing the marking of the ballot, De Armas is interested in dwelling into the reasons for the decision. Are you a Democrat when you vote Democrat? Are you a Republican when you vote Republican? The answer may be yes ... but not necessarily for the reasons you thought.

De Armas begins by shirking a quota of historical consensus, namely the stereotype that attaches to the Democratic Party more merit in the defense of civil rights than to the Republican Party. Something that many Republicans would have no problem admitting to, provided it was formulated in a different way. For example, the Democratic Party is responsible for a multicultural and multiethnic equivalency —relativistic— which has unanchored the nation from the universal values on which it was founded. But what De Armas points out is that, despite everything else, progress in civil rights matters should be as much, if not more, attributed to Republicans as opposed to Democrats.

Historically speaking, to give credence to the above, the author does a tour of American political writing, showing Republican contributions to the change in civil rights.

A similar exercise starts with the issue of immigration; particularly the illegal type generated at the southern border. De Armas simply dispatches as media propaganda the thesis that the Democratic Party is, as it is said, the Party of Immigrants. Without further ado, with regard to Latin American migrations in the 70s and 80s, the author recognizes the Reagan Administration for how it dealt with the effects of the phenomenon with its Immigration Reform and Control Act of 1986, which provided the broadest possible solution for the times. In contrast to this, he notes that President Obama, even having comfortable legislative control for two years achieved almost nothing in immigration matters.

Then a third public dogma goes through the crusher: that the Republican Party is the party of the rich, while the Democratic Party is for the less wealthy ones; with the usual uneven distribution of sympathies that a formally augmented value such as humility provides. Although at this point he could be expected to finish up, De Armas is in no hurry to impose conclusions and so he goes back to Andrew Jackson in search of enlightening events. One of them is the modern foundation of the Democratic Party as a "populist" machinery capable of consecrating these legends and political myths whose fallibility is one of the intellectual constants in the essayistic work of Armando de Armas; and not only in this essay *Cards in the Mirror*. His book *Myths of the Anti-Exile,* dedicated to "massacre" the label that the Cuban community in the USA has pasted on its own back, confirms this hypothesis.

Without wandering into sermons, and with notable humor, De Armas relies on checkbooks and checks to test relationships between money and political affiliation that reaches into the Bush-Kerry race. Finally, it must be said that the simple public image of President Obama does not fare well under the scrutiny of this essay.

Armando de Armas finishes his *Cards in the Mirror* with a meditation about the times, outlining an anthropology of our days to provide a backdrop for his own conclusions, because *Cards in the Mirror,* despite what has been mentioned, is not the work of an ideological Republican trying to bring down the Democratic Party; and not in the least to steal their voters. It is, as I was mentioning at the beginning, an effort to clean up the game; because, as the author says, "the problem would lie in the trick cards in place of playing with trick cards, in offending the intelligence of voters. The problem lies in demagoguery".

EMILIO ICHIKAWA
December 2011, Miami

CARDS IN THE MIRROR

Now we see but dimly, but then,
we will see face to face...
Letter of Saint Paul to the Corinthians

To Mimí, Andy, Amanda, Armando III and
Ariadna, also to Andy Armando, Anthony,
Omar, Angelina and Jesús Armando; with the
hope they will never see through a mirror

SOME UNSUSPECTING U.S. REACTIONARIES

Poker: Media handling of the cards

THE DEMOCRATIC PARTY MAY be the party of reaction in the United States. Not a problem if it were so. The problem would lie in the scam, almost always perpetrated by the media, to sell that party, at all costs, and sometimes in a trance, as a progressive party, when the facts would indicate exactly the opposite.

Let's take a look at history, Abraham Lincoln (February 12, 1809 April 14, 1865) was the 16th President of the United States and the first member of the Republican Party to become so; and, as a decidedly serious opponent of the expansion of slavery, Lincoln gained the nomination of his party in 1860 being elected president of the nation at the end of that year. During his administration he helped to preserve the political unity of the country defeating its enemies in the Civil War —with fierceness, it must be said!— the secessionist and pro-slave Confederate States of America, made up by eleven states in the South that had proclaimed their independence. The party of the secessionists and pro-slavery, let's be clear, was none other than the Democratic Party.

And so it is that the Democratic Party fought in that war to extend the reach of slavery, and not only that, but at the end of the fighting it was responsible for the establishment of Jim Crow laws, Negro Codes and repressive other laws that denied civil rights to American blacks. In this context is that in 1865 the first cell of the legendary and gloomy Ku Klux Klan is founded, grouping veterans of the Confederate Army who, after the War of Secession wished to resist the Reconstruction; a ten-year period in which African Americans were granted unprecedented political power in the South.

It is proper to clarify that the KKK was financed, supported and promoted by the Southern elites of the Democratic Party, and was not formally dissolved until 1870 by the then Republican President Ulysses S. Grant by way of the Civil Rights Act of 1871.

It must be said, additionally, that beginning in 1871 and up to 1930, in a desperate effort to deny civil rights and avoid having the Republicans vote in favor of them, thousands of African Americans were shot, beaten, lynched, mutilated and burned alive by members, now underground, of the Klan, and even worse: later on Democratic Presidents Franklin D. Roosevelt and Harry Truman would consistently refuse to sign laws against lynchings, one the one hand, and on the other opposing attempts to establish a Civil Rights Commission to permanently be on the lookout against flagrant violations of the civil rights of Negros.

On the other hand, the achievement of passing Constitutional Amendments 13, 14 and 15 which guarantee to U.S. blacks liberty, citizenship and the right to vote, in addition to the Civil Rights Acts of 1866 and 1875, which prohibit racial discrimination in public spaces is the handy work of the Republican Party.

And so, in the 1950s, Republican President and five-star WWII General Dwight David (Ike) Eisenhower championed the incorporation into the Army of minorities, decidedly supporting their civil rights. Republicans also passed the Civil Rights Act of 1957 (the main opponent that Ike encountered for its approval was none other than the then-leader of the Democrat majority in the Senate, and future president, Lyndon B. Johnson, who voted for an absolutely segregationist posture, until, forced by political circumstances, he finally ended up signing the Act of 1957, of 1964, and 1965 favoring those of African descent, additionally establishing Affirmative Action programs which would help Negros to prosper. These programs were proposed by Republican President Richard Nixon, in the so-called Philadelphia Plan of 1969 which opened the way for the Equal Opportunity Employment Act of 1972, which would finally make all affirmative action programs the law of the land. It is not even, we emphasize, that Affirmative Action is something truly progressive for blacks, something in fact debatable. The bottom line, in fact, is the advantage that inevitably is granted to Democrats for something that attaches, exclusively, to Republicans. And something similar has happened with illegal immigration from Latin America. The propaganda by the liberal media and Spanish-language radio and TV stations, induces those recent arrivals to Northern lands, subtly or openly, to vote Democrat, once their status is legalized, as the Democrats are the true defenders of La Raza ("The Race" is the name given here to those coming from south of the border, especially if they are Mexicans, and needless to say, the English-language media would have a fit if one day somebody would urge a vote in favor of The Race, and not from south of the border but rather The Race of the North, that is, the Anglo-Saxon Race, or even worse, the day when the Anglo-Saxons begin to call themselves The Race). But it turns out that beginning with the decade of the 1970s one of the largest migratory waves of all time swept into the United States; a wave coming mainly from Latin America, resulting in, among other things, that finally the decision is made to debate the matter in the U.S. Congress, considering various projects to legalize the undocumented. The undocumented arrive by the thousands from Mexico, Central America, Colombia, Peru, Argentina, Chile, Uruguay and Ecuador on account of the strong economic crisis in the region, as well as dictatorships, Communist subversion and drug trafficking.

Then, in 1986, during the presidency of Republican Ronald Reagan, the Immigration Control and Reform Act is passed, granting wide amnesty to those undocumented who complied with certain conditions, and as a result of it nearly 3 million immigrants applied for legal residency under said law. The truth is that 13 years later the number of illegals borders 12 million. Barack Obama and the Democrats were in full control of the House of Representatives and the Senate for two years, due, in part, to the fiery promises they made to 10 million Hispanic voters who played a decisive role in the 2008 presidential elections; the Latinos bet on Barack Obama by a 2 to 1 margin, giving him the victory in four states in which the Democratic candidate overtook the Republican Party, which where: Florida,

Colorado, Nevada and New Mexico. Obama then, and the Democrats, did nothing to emulate what Reagan and the Republicans had done in 1986, and even less were they to do after their crushing loss of the majority in the House of Representatives in 2010.

Even worse, according to a report by the Fair Immigration Reform Movement, the President of the United States, Barack Obama, has overtaken his predecessor George W. Bush in the number of illegal immigrants deported. The report points out that in the first year of the Obama Administration, the Immigration and Customs Enforcement Service deported 387,790 immigrants, an increase of 61.8% with respect to the average of 240,000 deported annually during the second Bush Administration. That is, we are talking about an average of 1,000 deportations a day in the Obama Administration, in contrast to 650 deported immigrants a day during the second Bush Administration.

The Civil Rights Act Card of 1964

As the storyline goes, there is a Democratic Party which began being reactionary and ended up being progressive, and a Republican Party which would have begun being progressive and has ended up reactionary. This magical metamorphosis would occur, definitively, when the Democratic Party and President John F. Kennedy were given the credit for the approval of the Civil Rights Act of 1964. Regardless, we should analyze, beyond the myth, what really took place.

In 1957, Kennedy, consistent with the traditional practice of his party, voted against the Civil Rights Act of 1963 opposing the massive march (some 200,000 people would participate) led by Reverend Dr. Martin Luther King Jr. in Washington, D.C. Later on Dr. King would harshly criticize Kennedy for ignoring the civil rights cause of the American Negro, and, in fact, he would always vote Republican.

The Civil Rights Act of 1964 was passed by Congress with 290 votes in favor and 130 against. Of the Republicans, 80% voted in favor of the new law. Of Democrats, 61% did the same. This means that only 20% of Republicans voted against the blacks, while among Democrats 39% voted against, double minus one point.

In the Senate the vote ended up 73 in favor of the law that favored blacks and 27 against. Only six Republicans voted against the law, compared to 21 Democrats who did the same. On July 2, 1964, Democrat President Lyndon Johnson signed the law, which, finally, would put pen to paper the equality of all United States citizens. These figures, regardless of how one looks at them, seem to point out that it would be more appropriate, or more fair, to say that the Civil Rights Act of 1965 was approved not by the Democrats, but despite the Democrats.

Interviewed by the author of this work, the then-U.S. Republican Congressman Lincoln Díaz-Balart stated that "it required great political courage on the part of Lyndon B. Johnson to decide for the important laws of 1964 and 1965" and that Kennedy did nothing in this regard. Díaz-Balart also added that "Johnson, before becoming president, had not supported the rights of African Americans, but that his leadership was key, now as president, to pass the laws of 64 and 65". It is proper to make clear that, in order to be balanced, Johnson's Republican opponent in the 1964 elections, and the author of the masterpiece work of U.S. conservatism *The Conscience of a Conservative,* Barry Goldwater, was definitively set against the 64 and 65 laws.

We also need to say that Democratic Senator Robert Byrd of West Virginia, a former member of the Ku Klux Klan, held a filibuster on the floor of the Senate in 1964, an obstructionist lengthy speech to hold the microphone, in a desperate attempt to block passage of the Civil Rights Act of 1964. Regardless, wonders you shall see, Senator Byrd was praised in April 2004 by Democratic Senator Christopher Dodd, as somebody who, had he had the opportunity, would have been, during the course of the Civil War, not a simple participant, no kidding around, but a great leader in favor of the cause… did he say pro-slavery? No siree bob, no way, of the slaves. That is what Dodd said, cavalierly acting as if he didn't know history; the story of Byrd.

By the way, amongst the Democrats who voted against the Civil Rights Act in 1964 was Senator Al Gore, father of the other Al Gore who was the Vice President during Bill Clinton's era, and the Democrat presidential candidate against George W. Bush in the year 2000 and a Nobel Peace Prize, presently, the latter in view of his efforts —dauntless and heroic, one must say! — to save Planet Earth from greenhouse gases and evil capitalists. We have no issue with being reactionary, we reiterate. The problem would lie in trick cards in place of playing with trick cards, in offending the intelligence of voters. The problem lies in demagoguery.

SOME UNSUSPECTED RICH AMERICANS

Andrew Jackson, Hooligan, Democrat and Freemason

THE DEMOCRATIC PARTY COULD increasingly be, as in the past, the party of the rich. I don't have a problem with the rich, without rich people there is no country. The problem would lie in the gyp, almost always by the press, of selling, at all costs, and at times in a trance, that it is the party of the poor, while the facts seem to contradict it.

The Democratic Party emerges as an offshoot of the old Democratic-Republican Party of the U.S. which governed uninterrupted from 1801 to when it entered into a crisis in 1824 because it was the first time that the election featured direct and universal suffrage and there were several presidential candidates calling themselves Democrat-Republicans and they all sought to claim the popular vote. One of these candidates was General Andrew Jackson, a legendary hero of the War of 1812 against the British, who lost the presidency despite having won the plurality of the popular vote, due to the process of the Electoral College which stipulates that if none of the candidates obtains an absolute majority, then Congress in session needs to select the president from among the candidates getting the most votes, and so it was that Congress elected John Quincy Adams. Then Jackson and his supporters began to found throughout the country chapters of a new party which at the time didn't have a definitive name; a party whose agenda would be precisely to take General Jackson to the presidency.

It's proper to point out, as a curious fact, that this new party could count on a formidable political party machine in the State of New York, inherited from the defunct Democratic-Republican Party, and that leveraging that, it became the first popular party —what we call today populist— in American history, mobilizing the masses and systematically taking advantage of a chain of sensationalist newspapers. This closeness with the press, something it has kept up even to this day, explains not only the effective and proverbial handling of public opinion by this group but also its ability, in a sort of game of mirrors, to appropriate for itself, more or less improperly, nice aspects and tendencies of the collective unconsciousness: and in the topic we are discussing, the virtue of poverty, deeply rooted in Christianity first, and abundant Marxist foliage later.

As a curiosity, let's say that Jackson was an eminent Freemason, a Great Master of the Tennessee Lodges, a controversial and brave man who had participated in duels several times, and who commanded the American forces which defeated the British at the Battle of New Orleans in 1815. In 1820, during the inaugural party, thousands of poor people were seen entering the White House in an unusual spectacle of pilgrimage. But this immersion with the masses would be short-lived as the new party, soon after General Jackson left the presidency in 1837, would increasingly drift away until it became the political party of the wealthy, slave-owning elites of the American South.

An Effective Political Marketing Operation

TRUTH BE TOLD, EVER since then, to define the Democratic Party as the party of the poor has never been anything but a stereotype. A political marketing operation effectively mounted, which would begin to decisively crumble beginning during the decades of the 1960s and 70s with the massive migration toward the Republican Party of ethnic minorities, low-income farmers, religious people, law-enforcement people, workers, women and Army veterans.

This was happening at the same time that large sectors of the wealthy class in the U.S., made up of bankers, men and women of the exclusive American academia, lawyers, powerful media moguls, new-rich millionaires and very famous Hollywood artists were migrating quickly and timely towards the Democratic Party.

For example, Donald Lambro published in *The Washington Times* on November 23, 2007, a study by Michael Franc, Vice-President for Government Relations for the Heritage Foundation, which, based on data from the Internal Revenue Service provides evidence that the wealthiest districts in the United States are Democrat fiefdoms. More than half of the districts with the highest income in the U.S. belong to 18 states where the Democrats control the both Senate seats. The study comes to this conclusion taking into account the number of individual contributors, which according to their income tax returns have income of $100,000 per year or higher, and of the number of couples whose returns show incomes of $200,000 or higher. We can say that the majority of households in Democrat districts earn around $49,000, a higher figure than the national average, which hovers around $40,000.

Thus, in the presidential elections of the year 2000, and according to a poll by Ipsos-Reid, if we were to compare counties voting in favor of Republican George W. Bush to those that voted for Democrat Al Gore, we can conclude that those that liked Bush were only 7% of voters earning more than $100,000, while 38% had incomes below $30,000. In contrast, in those countries favoring Gore 14% earned $100,000 or more while 29% earned less than $30,000.

On the other hand, the research of authors Robert Lichter, professor at George Mason University; Stanley Rothman, professor at Smith College; and Neil Nevitte, professor at the University of Toronto, published in the newspaper *The Washington Post* in March 2005, reflects that 72% of U.S. college professors declare themselves to be leftists or Democrat sympathizers, as compared with 15% who declare themselves rightists or Republican advocates.

The difference is even greater among instructors at the most exclusive schools, and therefore those that earn the most money, where 87% call themselves leftists against only 13% who confess to be right-wing.

Myths and Reality

IN THE IMAGINARY OF political correctness, George W. Bush would be, on account of his net worth and his party, a representative of the interests of the wealthiest of the nation. However, when the former president successfully ran for reelection in 2004, he declared a net worth between $8.1 and $21.5 million, certainly a ridiculously smaller figure as compared to the assets of his opponent, Massachusetts Democratic Senator John Kerry, who declared his at between $165.7 and $235.3 million. Additionally, according to U.S. press reports, Bush would leave the White House in 2008 with a $6.5 million decrease.

We are not saying that there are no poor people in the Democratic Party, or that there are no wealthy people in the Republican Party. What we are seeing is a trend whereby Democrats continue to move into the extreme millionaire elites, on the one hand, and towards the extreme of the poorest and those dependent on state aid, on the other hand, while Republicans are increasing their numbers among the so-called U.S. middle class. Therefore, at least financially speaking, in the first case we would be looking at a party that is bifurcating towards the margins, a party that is becoming Latin Americanized and which bipolarizes the use of social schemes of unreachable spaces between the very rich and the very poor as is the case south of the border, while in the second case we are looking at a party trending towards the center, and therefore, more representative of the national average, and what the United States is supposed to be: a first-world country.

Criton Zoakos, a financial consultant and President of Leto Research, states in a study that the middle class prefers fiscal, monetary and regulatory policies that favor free competition and wealth creation, while the high class prefers the preservation of their wealth and protection against competition through the use of high tax rates. The latter could explain why those possessing huge fortunes migrate to the Democrats, especially if these fortunes were inherited.

Finally, I have bad news for those that bought the story of a very humble Barack Obama, a storyline that would be reinforced by his wife Michelle who declared, plaintively, that she had come to feel proud of her country only after the election of her husband as a presidential primary candidate in 2008; with the subliminal understanding that the country, before then, had offered nothing to the couple. The truth of the matter is that the then-Democrat candidate to the White House and his wife earned $4 million during the prior year, according to the figures in their joint income tax return, later divulged by the campaign of the then-Illinois Senator. In fact, for being poor, it looks like the Obamas haven't done badly at all for themselves.

ZEITGEIST: THE SPIRIT OF THE TIMES

Politics

But the issue is not Barack Obama, nor is it his party; the problem is the kind of Politics that the times have wrought: Obama and his party as the greatest manifestation of the Politics of the day. The thing is that Politics in the West may have reached a turning point or a point of no return, spiritually speaking, beginning from the present Post-Modernity going back to the Renaissance, or it would cease to be Politics; and, therefore, the West would cease to be the West; or at least the West as we have known it for the last two millennia.

Just as the Renaissance signified, as far as possible, a return from the Middle Ages, understood as the last great era of humanity, towards Classical Antiquity, understood as the first great epoch of humanity, we could similarly be now entering a time-space hinge in which, as far as we can see, we would be returning to a Renaissance, not now from a great era but rather from a flatter one, so as not to exaggerate, from all similar times of humanity, which would grant a sense of urgency to this return: we return or we disappear, not as men, but as Western people; a people whose first concern would be freedom, and the individual's development.

A time when, contrary to the nonsense that abounds, the number of the poor in the world has dramatically decreased. Even in Latin America (a space that seems intent on repeating as a caricature of the worse in Europe, I am talking about Socialism in its several variations) there were at least 15 million people exiting poverty in 2006, according to numbers from the UN's agency for Latin America, CEPAL.But the problem is also related to the times, the Zeitgeist; one that could have begun to manifest itself after the Protestant Reform, but which initiate its universal and uniform escalation starting with the 19th century, entering its acceleration during the 20th, which would approach the definition of an oceanic climax in the first years of the 21st century. The Spirit of the Times is, as anyone who has suffered it or who has opposed it knows, socialistic and paternalistic, sensitive and mechanical, driving and taxing, seductive and implacable, offering solidarity and suicidal, rejecting of change and supporting planning; preferring redistribution of wealth to its creation, to talk about human rights as opposed to talking about the rights of the individual, to be submissive to war, to be moderate to freedom, weak men and strong women.

Want an example of the Spirit of the Time manifesting itself in Politics at the time of this writing? Here it goes: the international community, with the United States and the Obama Administration at the lead, removes sanctions against the regime of General Raúl Castro in Cuba, who blatantly declares that there will be no free and supervised elections, and so repeating what his brother, Castro number 1 said and did for half a century in the island, while, at the same time the same Obama was imposing very severe sanctions against the interim government in Honduras of Roberto Micheletti, who was desperately calling for free and supervised elections as the only way out of the national crisis at the time.

This Zeitgeist has imposed a new language, a meta-language coming from that which the late intellectual and Czech President Václav Havel correctly identified as the special language of the Communists which, he said, would be one of the more diabolical instruments for the enslavement of some and the entrancing of others.

And so, what is dangerous about this language, we say, is not that it was imposed or be imposed at the point of a gun to millions of human beings around the world under real Communism; but rather that this language has extrapolated its original and invalid context to the whole West, that it has demeaned opinion makers, and, what is worse, the masses who unarmed suffer under those opinion makers who construct opinions as witch doctors do, on account of the disproportionate development of the media and technology in the globalized era.A meta-language which in the process of not harming in the least the self-esteem of anybody has ended up damaging thought and creating a sort of new human, one who would be at the same time informed but dumb, docile and a moaner, anarchic and correct, comfortable and lacking in will. Under this Zeitgeist in the West we seem to be headed towards a society of beings induced by hypnopedia as in Aldous Huxley's *Brave New World*; a hypnopedia which in the words of one of its characters is described as the strongest moralizing and socializing force in History. It is a society of altruistic, anorexic, asexual beings, good speakers and even better thinkers. The Spirit of the Times first adopted the childish theories of a paradise on Earth which, only a few short years ago produced Nazi and Communist concentration camps and from whose memory it now flees in fear, in denial, to rewrite an amiable version of events, one where firing squads and death by gas would not be physical but rather mental and taking place not in camps but at dawn, if not on the screen and at any time, and where people equally depended on the daddy-state, the state-father as much as the father-god; it is what Pope Benedict XVI has come to define accurately as a center dictatorship.

Then, Politics needs to understand together with Czech writer Milan Kundera that today the only way to be modern, paradoxically, is to be anti-modern, that Post-Modernity with its relativism could be the easy way to take us not to the end of History, as Francis Fukuyama claimed, but rather to the end of civilization; at least as we have come to understand it in the West. Politics should be so wise, I mean so Renaissance, that it would learn from what is para-doxical par excellence, from the continuous interre-lationship between good and evil in the complexity of the world. It needs to come to a middle point in ethical balance, having enough wisdom, responsi-bility and courage to seek the good even at the risk of doing evil, or apparent evil; clearly, to understand with the greatest clarity that the case requires, that not always, and not in every circumstance, the dogma of faith is valid, probably Christian, which assures that the ends do not justify the means.

Politics, freed from oafs, needs to understand that it can, and at times has to, be unpopular, that a statesman who governs consulting polls is not a democrat, but rather very probably a dangerous demagogue, that the dialog of civilizations is not a dialog, it is a fairy tale, a long story (in fact multiple connected narratives) of *The One Thousand and One Nights,* where the frightened Scheherazade tries to seduce, by talking, Sultan Shahryar so that he, tired of listening to her, will not cut off her head with one stroke of his sword.

Politics, in order to prevail, as in the Renaissance, needs to bet more on the strength of the individual and less on the strength of the tribe, and, perhaps contradictorily, less on the fatherland and more on Western Civilization, for a Western Civilization we could all aspire to have as the ideal homeland. It is a fatherland threatened today as never before by militant Islamism and a plague of other –isms. Politics, as in the Renaissance, should not fear words, but also not actions. Politics is obliged to rescue the worth of the word liberty; as a matter of fact increasingly almost nobody talks about liberty anymore! Today's Politics cannot sidestep that the remnants of Communism have a powerful ally in Islamism; they are separated by a theocratic vision of the atheistic vision, but aside from that they are united in hate for the United States and the West.

The Man Without Qualities

THIS ZEITGEIST HAS GIVEN birth to a new specimen, and this specimen has a lot to do with the biped portrayed in the novel by Austrian Robert Musil (1880-1942) *The Man Without Qualities* a two-volume work between the years 1930 and 1943. This is probably one of the most ambitious novels ever written in German literature in the last century, as it is able to reflect without pity or hang ups the paradoxes of Modernity, about the crisis of Rationalism, and about the search for a theory and a praxis of feeling in order to reason about trapped emotions within a system that has been asphyxiated by science and the complexity and complications of life.

A biped who, with a seriously damaged psyche, submits submissively to the disproportionate state machinery of the supra-Modernity embedded in Fascism and Communism so as to, after the liberation that meant the triumph of the allies after the Second World War, emerged even more damaged, not now in its psyche but in the psyche and body, and in the soul, but mostly in the soul. An entity ready on the one hand to inhabit the Gulag of the Soviets and on the other hand to inhabit the Gulag of the media, that which in some way had been foreshadowed and wished for by the intellectual Antonio Gramsci (1891-1937) and which now manifests itself beyond the lands of what used to be the Iron Curtain.

The Spirit of the Times has blown not only to take Barack Hussein Obama to the White House, but also for him to be given the Nobel Peace Prize for his worthy promises.

It is the same wind that blew, but in the opposite direction, so that Jorge Luis Borges, probably the greatest writer born in the Western Hemisphere, was never given the Nobel for Literature. With the Nobel Peace Prize, Obama sets a terrific precedent for the Nobel Prize in Literature. In the future it could be awarded to a writer of promise, hand over heart, who promises to write extraordinary and renewing novels, senses and revolutionary poems.

BARACK HUSSEIN OBAMA, OR THE GOLDEN BOY OF THE U.S. POLITICAL IMAGINARY

Oba Facing the Board of Ifa

OBA, AS SOME MAY know, is the sovereign and priest of the Yoruba nation, tribes which were originally located in territories now Chad and in Upper Egypt, flourishing as a culture around the 12th century in West Africa, especially in the holy city of Ife, under the auspices of the Ifa religion of southeast Nigeria.

Barack Obama is not a sovereign, he was a Democrat Senator and later President, but a U.S. Senator, not to mention as president, has a lot of power, lots more than was ever dreamt by the proud little kings of Yoruba lands.

Obama is also not a practitioner of Ifa, he is not even a Catholic; Obama is said to have been a Muslim and now a Protestant. In fact, not even his paternal ancestors, on account of being black, come from Nigeria but rather from Kenya, on the other side, in East Africa. These facts may go a long way in explaining his feelings of being uprooted, and the problems of integration, not just of Obama —who is not even a Negro, he is a Mulatto—, but also of large sectors of the U.S. black population as compared to the greater rootedness and integration of the black Latin American population, especially in the Caribbean. We are emphasizing the unequal difficulties, disagreements, frictions and violence, in a word the estrangement that a forced immigration, subjected to slavery in an environment and in a world not only absolutely unknown, but also absolutely hostile; the key jump, mostly deadly, from the Stone Age to the Modern Age, would frankly have been made acute in the lands of Anglo-Saxon colonialism on account of some almost insurmountable psychological and social breaks inflicted due to the passage, without a transition, from polytheism, in some cases, and poly-demonism in most —that held sway in African tribes— into the fiercest monotheism of Protestants in the Anglo-Saxon tribe.

This situation would be buffered in lands under Iberian monarchies where there was, despite the Black Legend espoused by English Protestantism, a greater tolerance with the mixing, not only sexual, but also in religion, where Catholicism, with its profusion of virgins and saints for each daily problem, was in practice a sort of low-grade polytheistic religion, which, with ecclesiastical acquiescence, allowed blacks to accommodate or camouflage their spirits and *orishas* behind virgins and saints.

These marked characteristics would determine, probably, the lesser degree of racial integration in the British colonial system as compared with the Iberian one, the evident idiosyncratic differences of attitude to life and society of blacks in one milieu in contrast with the other.

Many of the stumbles experienced by the then-Senator Barack Obama during his campaign to obtain the nomination of the Democratic Party for the presidency of the United States would have had their probable antecedent in the way British colonists related to blacks, both in North America as in Africa itself (let's not forget that the paternal ancestors of the president come from what was an enclave of British colonialism) and that on the other hand, the way in which blacks reacted when facing the Anglo-Saxon model after independence, the abolition of slavery, the struggle for civil rights, and even in the present, to the sequels of the former imperial relationships that still persevere and reappear in strength, after periods of apparent normality. That reaction has been channeled and is being channeled, in a way such that a wide spectrum of the U.S. black population does not feel identified with the nation which was left in inheritance by the founding fathers, but rather feel uprooted and in extreme cases enemies of the very complex skein which historically has configured the United States.

The adoption of Islam by a portion of the U.S. black population (42% of the three million domestic Muslims are blacks born in the country, according to figures from the American Muslim Council) and the use of terms such as African Americans, and more recently, of African descent, as well as the use of tattoos with the Maori symbol in the hardened face of former heavy-weight champion boxer Mike Tyson, would have their probable beginnings in an ancestral psycho-social discontent and the desperate search for an identity, no matter how hallucinating it could seem, or outside the national ethos, outside of the Western culture that is logically predominant in the United States.

How else to explain the issues the former Senator from Illinois had on account of his frankly anti-U.S. relationships. The case of his pastor and spiritual guide for more than twenty years, the angry Jeremiah Wright, the same who officiated the Obama wedding, one and the same who later baptized his daughters, and who has stated and reiterated at the National Press Club that the terrorist attacks on 9/11 in New York were justified because the United States was a terrorist nation, and because the U.S. government had invented in its laboratories the AIDS virus as a way to conduct genocide on people of color, and that consequently, it was natural for God to damn the U.S., adding that he, as a pastor, spoke what he was thinking, saying the truth, but that it was natural for politicians such as Obama to only say what was convenient for them, would lie, thus explaining in front of the press the distance that the Democrat President had taken from this spiritual mentor.

Only by analyzing things in this fashion is that we can acquire a certain sense of the friendship between Barack Obama and terrorists William Ayers and Bernardine Dohrn, who together between 1969 and 1975 headed up a group called the Weather Underground, which committed dozens of attacks and violent crimes in the U.S.

Michelle Obama has declared, as we already mentioned, publicly and solemnly, with the serenity of someone who is saying something totally natural, that the nomination of her husband had made her proud to be from the United States for the first time in her life. That is, that before this day Mrs. Obama felt humiliated at being an American, despite the fact that that society with which she evidently didn't feel at home, had provided to both her and to Barack the opportunity to study in the most exclusive schools and that they would earn combined, according to their tax return made known by the campaign of the then-candidate to the presidency, the not-too-shabby amount of $4 million during the year previous to his campaign for the White House, as we mentioned before.

And now we are entering the topic of Obama's fortune, as we note another of the stumbling blocks of his 2008 presidential campaign, also related to his lack of identification, but this time not due to the sequels left on African Americans due to British colonialism, but this time on account of his alienation due to his being in an intellectual and wealth elite to which Obama and his entourage surely belong. The stumbling block happened before the Pennsylvania primary when the then-Senator expressed, regarding people in rural small towns who had lost their jobs: "And it's not surprising then they get bitter, they cling to guns or religion or antipathy toward people who aren't like them or anti-immigrant sentiment or anti-trade sentiment as a way to explain their frustrations." A statement that would indicate not only his estrangement but also his absolute lack of knowledge about the nation which he governed for eight years; because the two unassailable basis upon which the American Union was erected are, precisely, the citizen's right to own, bear and shoot guns, on the one hand, and the right to freedom of religion, on the other.

Obama forgets that both rights appear in *The Bill of Rights* which was signed December 15, 1791, which really define the United States, and without which the Constitution would have never been signed as the Supreme Law of the land. Obama forgets that to relate economic issues with faith, and faith as the consequence of economic problems, has more to do with the Marxist maxim that religion is the opium of the people than with the fact that we are talking about a people who had the words In God We Trust printed on their currency. Obama forgets that most of the architectural and artistic monuments of humanity we owe more to religion and to opulence than to economic issues.

A legend tells that once an Oba was elected in the holy city of Ife, after going through the rituals facing the divination board of Ifa, the deity needed to speak under the sign of Obara, a word I would translate as "the King that doesn't lie" followed by the refrain: *The dog has four paws but takes only one road.* This would augur a good government for the kingdom, because the sign and the refrain were referring basically to the fact that the Oba would side with the truth and he would know how to conciliate, from his place in the power structure as a celestial body or Mandala, the actual four corners of the kingdom. It was all that the Yoruba asked of their proud sovereigns.

Obama's Second Term

AT THE TIME OF the second edition of this book many of the trends pointed out in the first in 2011 inside the Democrat and Republican machineries, and in the American society in general, not only still hold but are also going on and being reaffirmed.

And so, Barack Obama turns out to have deported the most undocumented Latinos in decades. But, truth be told, Hispanics do not show much inclination to feel offended by his record of deportations and as proof note how they supported Hillary Clinton in her race for the White House. The former Secretary of State received the endorsement of the Congressional Hispanic Caucus in February 2016, and a poll taken on that same date regarding the Latino vote and broadcast by Univision and *The Washington Post,* revealed good news for the former Secretary of State: 57% of Latinos in the whole country support her, while 28% support her opponent in her own party, Bernie Sanders, and so we would be talking about 85% of Hispanics would side with the Democrat option. In April, the Latino leadership in The Bronx closed ranks in favor of Clinton, "a friend of the community that will make history as the first woman president in this country", according to the text of the press release.

Following the trend identified in the first edition, Obama, before finishing his two terms surpassed his predecessors for several decades, with figures of approximately 3 million undocumented Latinos deported to their home countries from the United State, according to data from the Homeland Security Department. And so, due to that drive of expulsions, some critics within the Latino community dared to call Obama the Deporter-in-Chief. The term was adjudicated in 2014 to Janet Murguía, President of the National Council of La Raza, already mentioned in the previous edition. "Obama is the one who has deported the most. The numbers support that. For the President, I think his legacy is at stake here" the activist added. "There is a stain, a black cloud" over his legacy, she added. Therefore, in comparison, in his eight-year term, evil Bush deported about 2 million undocumented, or, a million less that good old Obama. And so, Isabel García, from Arizona, Director of the Legal Defender's Office in Pima County, in the Tucson area, founder of the National Migrant's Rights Network, and first foreigner to win the National Human Rights Prize in Mexico, with her pedigree obviously a person not to be suspected as having rightist inclination, doesn't cower when declaring to the *ABC* newspaper in Spain: "Obama has deported more migrants than any other president in U.S. history".

Therefore, we would have to say that Republican George Bush in his eight years in the White House had what was probably the most diverse and multiethnic

Government in American history, including, among others, the following African Americans, Red Paige in Education, retired general Colin Powell as Secretary of State, as well as Condoleezza Rice who was first National Security Advisor and later U.S. Secretary of State, the latter a historical milestone without precedent in American society, and never acknowledged by the national press, which came before the historical milestone of the election of Obama as the first black president, repeated *ad nauseum* by the same media. In addition to Condoleezza Rice, another five women were nominated to his Cabinet (and feminist activists never praised Bush): Ann Veneman, Secretary of Agriculture, Christine Todd Whitman, head of the Environmental Protection Agency, Gale Norton at Interior, and Hispanic Linda Chávez, Labor Secretary, who was forced to resign presumably for paying another Hispanic, an illegal woman, for working as a maid in her home, forcing Bush to nominate Elaine Chao, an Asian and former official in the Ronald Reagan and George H.W. Bush administrations, who was confirmed by the Senate. He also had in his staff Cubans such as Mel Martínez and Carlos Gutiérrez, the former in the Dept. of Housing and Urban Development and the latter as Commerce Secretary, in addition to Mexican American Alberto Gonzales, first White House Attorney and later Attorney General of the U.S. who fought off strong opposition from the Democrats before being finally confirmed to this post. There was even a Democrat in Bush's cabinet, Secretary of Transportation Norman Mineta, also Asian, who had previously held the job of Secretary of Commerce under Bill Clinton.

But, aside from the deportations, in July 2014 a survey conducted by the prestigious Quinnipiac University in Connecticut assured us that Obama had been categorized as the worst U.S. president since WWII as 33% of those polled named Obama when asked who they considered to have been the worst president to date, followed by 28% who mentioned Bush, Jr., who had been the victim of an unprecedented negative media campaign, followed by 13% for Richard Nixon, who due to the Watergate Scandal had been the only president to resign in the history of the country. "In the last 69 years of U.S. history and 12 presidencies, President Barack Obama joins George W. Bush with the lowest popularity," explained Tim Malloy, Associate Director of the Quinnipiac Poll. On the other hand, 35% pointed to Ronald Reagan (1981-1989) as the best president since 1945.

In comparing the presidencies of Bush (2001-2009) and Obama, only 39% of those polled show a favorable opinion to the current president, while 40% favored the Bush years. This fact is surprising in as much as Obama arrived at the White House with a very high favorability rating, the darling of the press and of opinion leaders worldwide, and with the stated promise of being different from the Bush Administration, characterized by the unpopular wars in Iraq and Afghanistan. In addition, the poll showed that 45% of the country thought that the country would be better off if Republican Mitt Romney had won the 2012 elections.

The Obama Administration has been a disaster in foreign policy, especially in the complicated area of the Middle East. American historian and political scientist Daniel Pipes, President of the Middle East Forum, is of the belief that with Obama the U.S. has fallen into a tremendous irrelevance in this whole region, and that inconsistency, incompetence and inaction have made his Government impotent. In the international political scene the president acts as if he would prefer to be the Prime Minister of Belgium, a small nation which, habitually, copies the decisions of its larger neighbors when voting at the United Nations, or remains morally aloof respecting far-away issues. Thus, we affirm that Obama, be it due to ineptitude or be it due to contempt for what the U.S has been up to now seems to act more like an enemy than as a friend of the worldwide interests of the nation he represents. How else to explain his rapprochement with Iran and his estrangement with Israel, America's most trusted ally in the globe, and the only trust-worthy one in that region. Obama has given the impression of being more interested in a statist U.S. through his Obamacare and tax increases than to guarantee U.S. hegemony in the world, and thus National Security. Analyst Kim Holmes and academic William Inboden at the University of Texas, Austin, point out in their new strategy handbook for public policy for Congress, published by Heritage Action for America, that "our situation is really grave. Once again, terrorism menaces our homeland. As we have backed out of the world, numerous territories have fallen into chaos and turned into terrorist training grounds. The administration has committed too many unforced errors: like leaving Iraq too quickly (and probably Afghanistan as well); staying out of the

Syrian conflict until a point when it was impossible to turn aside; deciding to forego obtaining crucial intelligence by killing terrorists with drones rather than interrogating them; like freeing detainees from Guantánamo, which have returned to the battle"… And the authors continue by pointing out that these "errors emanate from a myopic vision that states that we are not really at war against terrorism. Not even the French believe that any more"… "Although these are the most obvious problems, there is a much greater one, it is bandied about that the United States is trying to stop being a superpower. The main reason is Obama's lack of commitment to being a world leader, which could be clearly felt when he didn't send anyone with the rank of ambassador to the march against the *Charlie Hebdo* massacre in Paris. Our perceived weakness is now part of everybody's playbook. Our neglected allies are beginning to look for other types of protection. Enemies and rivals see opportunities that would have been unimaginable six years ago."

Due to Obama's foreign policy, America's enemies and their allies have been empowered and are on the move. The total collapse of the established order in the Western world after the victories in the Second World War in 1945, and the Cold War in 1989, seems to be a real possibility in Europe. Experts in foreign policy in Washington were substituted by academics with little practical experience, and so the enemies of America and of the Western world cannot help but be pleased. The so-called sympathy that Obama enjoys abroad is actually their gladness at seeing the arrival of an anti-American to the White House, of someone that they see as a golden opportunity to advance their agendas.

But Obama, who is naïve, or acts like one, thinks he is in control. "You asked me about the Obama Doctrine. That Doctrine is simple: we commit, but without losing any of our capabilities", said Barack Obama to Thomas Friedman, a journalist at *The New York Times* whom he had invited to the Oval Office in the White House to explain his reasoning for the history agreement with Iran (because, let's not forget, that for Obama everything is historic, no matter what or at what price), and then he added: "For example, Cuba. We can try the possibility of an agreement that will have positive results for the Cuban people without great risk to us. It is a small country (...) And if later it turns out that it doesn't lead to anything good, we can always adjust our policy," he pontificated in an academic tone of voice, ignoring, or trying to ignore, that all that regimes such as Cuba or Iran need is time, a lot of time, and then will see.

Obama continued: "The same can be said about Iran. It is a large country, dangerous, which has taken part in activities that have resulted in the death of American citizens. But what is a fact is that Iran's defense budget is $30 billion while ours is nearing $600 billion. Iran knows that it cannot fight against us."

But what seems to be true about the Obama Doctrine turns out to be nothing more than throwing overboard the undeniable American military superiority to take the chance of following diplomacy to its logical conclusion, and this is, as was the case with Cuba and

Iran, to hand it all in return for nothing, to keep the enemy happy, so as, to be sure, he will not be angry at us, which subliminally would mean that the enemy is bad because we have previously provoked him or perhaps we have been unfair to him, but if we fatten him up and if we indulge him, well then, he will remain placidly and pleasantly within his borders. Because, Obama believes, in the end he can always appeal to war if all else has failed, that is, by the time it is too late and they are already at our kitchen. Thus, Obama took more steps than any other president to end two of the longest and more complex U.S. foreign policy conflicts, Cuba and Iran.

That Cuba continues to be a present danger for the U.S. is obvious, as can be gathered from the testimony offered in February 2015 by various experts attending a hearing on *The President's New Cuba Policy and U.S. National Security* at the Subcommittee on Western Hemisphere Affairs of the House of Representatives.

The hearing was called by the Chairman of the Subcommittee, Jeff Duncan (R, South Carolina), with the participation of Albio Sires (D-New Jersey), Ileana Ros-Lehtinen (R-Florida), Gregory Meeks (D-New York), Ron DeSantis (R-Florida), Joaquin Castro (D-Texas), Matt Salmon (R-Arizona), Christopher Smith (R-New Jersey) and Ted Yoho (R-Florida).

The witnesses recalled past and present activities, secret and public, developed by the Cuban Communist Government against the United States to alter the balance of power in the hemisphere.

In the historical aspect, sending Cuban officers to Vietnam to interrogate American POWs, the safe harbor offered to members of terrorist organizations such as the Basque ETA, and the Colombian FARC, as well as fugitives from justice accused of millionaire Medicare fraud and terrorists such as Joanne Chesimard, on the FBI's Ten Most Wanted List, who, up to this day, continue to live in the island despite extradition requests and the normalization of diplomatic relations between both countries.

As part of the current activities against U.S. security and that of the world, which continue going on today, an exposition was made of how Cuba exports military, police and intelligence advisors to control, watch, repress and kill unprotected Venezuelans in the course of implanting Socialism, as well as holding meetings with Russia to reopen the radio electronic surveillance base at Lourdes, Cuba, and the welcoming of spy ships into Cuban harbors.

For example, the issuance of 173 Venezuelan passports to Islamist elements to enter Canada, the secret weapon shipment to North Korea, the sale —or the sharing— of U.S. secrets to governments such as Iran, Syria and Russia and the recruitment and infiltration of spies at the highest spheres of the U.S. Government.

Christopher Scott Simmons, having more than 20 years of experience as U.S. Army counterintelligence officer and at the Defense Intelligence Agency, explained the importance of keeping in mind the threat of Cuban espionage for U.S. National Security.

Simmons, who was part of one of the most successful counterintelligence operations in the U.S. towards Cuba between 1996 and 2004, and who played a key role in the case against Castro spy Ana Belén Montes, and who was the officer in charge of expelling 14 Cuban diplomats working as spies in 2003, stated that underestimated and misunderstood for more than half a century, the Government in Havana continues to be a clear and present danger for the United States. Its Army and Intelligence organs exist exclusively to ensure the continuity of the regime, Simmons reasserted, while explaining that the Cuban espionage services are fed reports regarding millions of people who belong to the Committees for the Defense of the Revolution (CDR) which means that Cuban Intelligence is in fact 34 times greater than the Intelligence Service Community of the United States.

Cuban espionage focuses on two points: the Cuban people and the United States, and one of its three agencies, the Directorate of Intelligence (DI) is considered to be the fifth or sixth best intelligence service in the world.

Havana is recognized as an intelligence trafficker around the world, which sells or negotiates secret information stolen from the United States, said Simmons, adding that these activities report profits valued in the hundreds of millions of dollars in cash, goods, and services for the regime.

The expert in counterintelligence cited five aspects of the new policy by President Barack Obama towards Cuba that could be conducive to a greater threat to U.S. National Security:

- Injecting capital into the Cuban Intelligence and Security services with the profit made from trips by Americans to the island.

- Facilitating better opportunities to evaluate and recruit U.S. travelers willing to betray their country.
- Providing them with unlimited access to U.S. technology which would enhance the technological capabilities of the Cuban espionage and repression agents.
- Eliminating travel restrictions for diplomats/spies living in the U.S. The most notable was the opening of the Cuban Embassy in the U.S., consulates (in 1961 Cuba had 28 consulates in the U.S.) and the offices of the press agency Prensa Latina (which already has correspondents in New York, Washington, Chicago, Los Angeles, San Francisco, Miami, Denver and Atlanta.)
- Feeding the myth that Cuba no longer constitutes a menace for the U.S., something proclaimed by the regime five decades ago.

Simmons concluded that the strengthening of relations with Cuba will increase as never before the efficacy and the advancement of the Cuban intelligence services.

A similar scrutiny was made by Congresswoman Ileana Ros-Lehtinen, who enumerated several actions by the regime in Havana against the United States: the shooting of the civilian airplanes of Brothers to the Rescue, conversations with the Russians to reopen their espionage facilities at Lourdes, Cuba, the authorization of Russian spy ships to enter Cuban waters, the contraband of arms with North Korea, the granting of sanctuary to U.S. fugitives from the law and to

FARC and ETA terrorists, as well as military training in Venezuela.

She also underlined that the Castro regime has penetrated the U.S. espionage service with spies such as Ana Belén Montes and Kendall Myers. She recalled the presence of Cuban agents in the torture sessions endured by American prisoners of war in North Vietnamese prison camps such as The Zoo, and their ties to Iran, Russia and Syria.

The Cuban American Congresswoman finished by saying that President Obama should learn from history that negotiating with the Castro regime is a futile effort.

A year later, in February 2016, the Director of U.S. National Intelligence James Clapper, testified before the Senate's Armed Forces Committee that, and especially in its espionage service, Cuba is a real threat to the internal security of the United States. In his annual report to Congress, this high official declared that the menace posed by foreign intelligence services —both state as non-state actors— is persistent, complex and in evolution.

"Russia and China represent the greatest menace, followed by Iran and Cuba," explained Clapper to the audience. Despite the reestablishment of diplomatic relations on December 17, 2014, Cuban espionage has not ceased to hold the U.S. as its main enemy, Clapper added.

The regime in the island seems hell bent on trafficking in arms with countries that are enemies of the U.S., we say, because in addition to the case of the North Korean ship full of Cuban weapons in Panama in July 2013, which included parts for two MiG-21 airplanes, two anti aircraft missile systems, RPG rocket launchers, short-reach rockets, explosives, ammunition and missile control commands and grenades, in February 2015 the Chinese ship *Da Dan Xian* was detained at the Port of Cartagena, Colombia, suspected of transporting arms illegally to Cuba, when it was found inside its cargo 100 tons of powder, 2,640,000 charges, 99 projectile nuclei and around 3,000 shells to build artillery cannons.

At the present time, April 15, 2016, the media is reporting that Panama's National Police has confiscated 401 packs of cocaine inside a container arriving from Cuba; however, a high Panamanian official was quick to add that the drugs could have been loaded at the Panamanian port of Colón. "The contamination could have occurred at the port", said the Minister of Public Security, Rodolfo Aguilera by telephone to the TV show A Fondo in Miami's America TeVe. The official added that the container was aboard the ship *MSS Canberra*.

The shipment was found in a container at the Port of Colón, during an operation named Caña Brava. According to the Panamanian Police, the cocaine bundle was hidden inside tanks of molasses.

Curiously, the North Korean ship mentioned in the above report, the *Chong Chon Gang*, was also stopped when finding 240 tons of weapons coming from Cuba hidden under a shipment of sugar, as if the island regime was using the same modus operandi to hide its contraband passing through Panama, hiding them in the dark and in the sweet, a poisoned candy to outwit the Panamanian brethren —Sweeeeeeeet! as the late singer Celia Cruz would say in Spanish azúuuuuuuuuucar!— but this time, Minister of Public Security, it could not have been the Panamanians doing it themselves.

After the North Korean ship's incident, the UN determined that Cuba had violated the weapons embargo which that organization had imposed on the Asian nation, but the matter didn't have much consequences for the regime in the island, nor will it have as in the case of the ship filled with drugs because, as we know, Cuba is not a danger to anyone.

The 2016 Primary Candidates

WITH RESPECT TO THE mythological herd of rich, racist and reactionaries Republicans, on the one hand, and the racially sensitive, progressive and near-to-the poor Democrats, on the other hand, the faces and the banking accounts of the primary candidates in both parties that were still around campaigning in March 2016, should speak for themselves to any alert and impartial observer. While Republicans had two Hispanics of Cuban origin, Marco Rubio, 44 and Ted Cruz, 45 and two whites, John Kasich, 63 and Donald Trump, 69, the Democrats had two candidates as white as two snow dolls at Christmastime, Hillary Clinton, 68 and Bernie Sanders, 74. To complete the multiracial panorama of the Republicans we should add that in addition black doctor Ben Carson, 64 was part of the competition until he quit at the beginning of March.

Now let's sniff around a bit into the bank accounts of the primary candidates in both parties. According to *Forbes* magazine, Donald Trump is by far the wealthiest of all those competing in the 2016 elections. He is the despised Lone Ranger of the Republican Party, and his fortune tops $4.5 billion. The controversial real estate magnate got the attention of the audience several times during the Republican presidential debate in the United States, and, paradoxically, he is not even a Republican in the conventional sense of the word.

The former State Secretary Hillary Clinton sits in second place with a fortune of $45 million.

Bernie Sanders would be the poor man of the Democrats with a net worth of $700,000 and a $100,000 house. According to estimates by columnist Fernán Martínez Mahecha, Sanders is at the 86th ranking in wealth among U.S. Senators and he is 47 times poorer than Hillary, and 230 times poorer that the couple Bill and Hillary, and 7.8 times better off than the average American family. But according to our calculations, he is much more wealthy than right-wing Republican Marco Rubio (with a net worth of $100,000) who arrived at the Senate as the young promise of the even more right-wing popular movement, the Tea Party.

The figure that is probably most presidential and conservative among Republicans is Ted Cruz, with his $3.5 million, does not exactly stand out for his wealth. Lastly, the weakest of the Republican primary candidates, John Kasich, has amassed a fortune of $10 million.

Sanders, positioned to the left of Obama, to the point that he honeymooned with his first wife… in Hawaii?; nope, not at all, in the former and desalinated Soviet Union, traveling to Nicaragua to protest against U.S. backing for the Contra rebels declaring in a 1985 interview in a video that Fidel Castro educated children and transformed Cuban society; of course, what he doesn't mention in the video is how he transformed it. The Brooklyn native would be the only Socialist among the primary candidates, or at least the only one to self-proclaim it, and as a Socialist he doesn't blush at all when stating that where he to get to the Oval Office he would plunder with taxes above 50% the very wealthy, and that he would forbid the possession of assault firearms in the U.S., offering free college education, raising the minimum wage to $15, granting Medicare to all, forcing U.S. companies to return home, penalizing with taxes those companies that emit smoke, designating millions of dollars from taxpayers to, according to him, lower the sea level, protecting the planet and, more modestly, the ecosystem of the Great Lakes, stopping oil drilling, forcing banks to lend money to small businesses, championing more rights for homosexuals, bisexuals, transsexuals, and lesbians, ruining the DEA, fiercely fighting against the so-called global warming, legalizing abortion, prohibiting the death penalty, making the use of marijuana and alcohol the same, ending the supposed racial discrimination in the legal system, supporting the peace treaty with Iran's regime and legalizing the undocumented.

And so, if he were elected, this super friend of the poor would not only make them poorer but also he would make poorer those that are wealthy. And the love of this Socialist Sanders for the disinherited from fortune would be so fabulous that he would triple them in a jiffy with his wise solutions. What is curious here is the progressive Sanders, who is not only very old but is also defending ideas that are much older even, is being followed, to the envy of the other primary candidates in both parties, by crowds of youth that idolize him fearlessly; another evidence undoubtedly, of American decadence.

Let's Go Over Hillary Clinton

LET'S NOSE AROUND A bit on the financial handlings and problems of Progressive Hillary. In a recent interview, journalist Diane Sawyer of the ABC TV network dared to question if the $5 million ($100 million in the case of his august husband) she had earned with her speeches was not too much money. "We left the White House totally broke," she replied, completely immutable, the friend of the poor, blacks and Hispanics in this world. When Sawyer reminded her that that those $5 million are ten times the median annual salary of an American, the Democrat declared without skipping a beat that they had debts, that they had mortgages to be paid, and that they also had to pay for the education of daughter Chelsea, adding that oh my goodness they have to earn twice as much to buy their houses.

Going beyond what the former Secretary of State said, the couple spent $1.7 million on a mansion in an area of multimillionaires north of New York City. Then these social warriors spent $2.85 million on the purchase of another mansion in a rich suburb of Washington, D.C., and, in the year 2000, the Democrat primary candidate was getting a small advance of $8 million for her biography. During the twelve months that followed his exit from the presidency her husband, good ole Bill, pocketed the pocket change of $13 million for his speeches. By the year 2004, all debts had disappeared, and the money kept on coming in. When she arrived at the position of Secretary of State in 2009, the married couple declared a net worth in excess of $50 million.

In January 2016, Fox News was reporting that the U.S. Federal Bureau of Investigation was investigating the use of a private email server by Hillary Clinton while conducting official business, in order to determine if there was any crime of corruption in her messaging while handling classified information or affecting national security. According to Fox News, which was citing three intelligence sources, the FBI wanted to know if there was a possible intersection between the work of the Clinton Foundation and her work at the Department of State which could have transgressed public anti corruption laws. "Agents are investigating the possible intersection of donations to the Clinton Foundation, the handing out of contracts by the State Department and if normal procedures were followed", stated a source mentioned by Fox.

The report by the network came out after several news stories had been published the previous year about a possible mixing of activities by Hillary between the State Department and the Clinton Foundation, a charitable organization founded by her husband Bill. According to the network, the Foundation received donations and grants worth north of $144 million in 2013. One of the intelligence sources told Fox News that "many previous corruption cases have come up and have been successfully prosecuted with much less evidence than what is coming up in this investigation". What is certain is that neither the FBI nor the State Department has publicly commented on the Fox report.

The scandal about the emails exploded in 2015, just when Clinton was getting ready to launch her presidential run, and that is when the media revealed that she had used her private account for matters of national business while she headed up U.S. diplomacy.

Thousands of Clinton emails have been made public by order of a federal judge, Rudolph Contreras, who instructed the State Department to publish monthly, until January 2016, the emails of the Democrat primary candidate. The President of the Republican National Committee, Reince Priebus, wrote on Twitter that the news coming out in Fox News was disquieting. Priebus added that "favoritism towards donors to the Clinton Foundation from her own State Department is undeniable".

FIFA (the world soccer federation), which has of late been plagued by corruption scandals, is a partner of the Clinton Foundation on numerous initiatives, as reported by *The Daily Beast* in May 2015. The amount of the donations that FIFA sent to the Clinton Foundation figures in the list of donors of the federation. According to FIFA, the Clinton Foundation received in 2014 donations worth between $250,000 and $500,000 from the Qatar 2022 World Cup Committee. The foundation also has received donations valued at between $1 and $5 million from the Government of Doha.

And so, while pro-democracy protests were congregating in the streets of Cairo in 2011, facing death to oppose the government of Hosni Mubarak, the then-Secretary of State was presenting herself as a defender of human rights assuring us to be "deeply worried about the use of violence on the part of the police and of Egyptian security forces against the demonstrators". But Hillary was playing another game behind the scenes, according to a June 2015 report by the *International Business Times*. On the one hand she was warning the White House about the importance of the resignation of President Mubarak, whom she had previously called a great friend of the family. While on the other hand, the State Department, headed up by her was persuading Egypt to purchase arms from the U.S. Government, classified as toxicological agents, which includes chemical and biological weapons, which were slowly utilized by Mubarak forces against the demonstrators which were demanding his destitution, according to the publication.

And so, the approval to export chemical and biological products to the Egyptian Government by the State Department, managed by Hillary Clinton, that untiring defender of the humble, kept increasing as the flow of dollars kept flowing into the Foundation. A group closely attached to the Mubarak Government paid good ole Bill $250,000 in 2010, some four months before the start of the Egyptian revolt.

All seems to indicate that the approval for the American chemical weapons to Egypt was directed to benefit the interests of the Clinton family, mostly in cash; a sample of the use of power to obtain millions in revenues.

And so, in two years of protests during the Arab Spring, with popular uprisings which confronted some governments, the Clinton State Department approved the sale of $66 million in arms exports to the region. These weapons were sold to nine governments in the Middle East.

In June 2015, *The Washington Times* conducted an investigation showing that a branch of the Clinton Foundation in Sweden received $26 million, at the same time that Stockholm was pressuring the former Secretary of State to eliminate sanctions on Iran. According to several documents and reports cited in the investigation, the matter was never known by the State Department, since all the paperwork was done and registered in Sweden.

Numerous Swedish international companies, such as Ericsson and Volvo, were against the strict sanctions imposed against the Persian dictatorship because of their own commercial interests, while, for all of them, Iran was the second-largest market in the Middle East for Swedish exports after Saudi Arabia.

The inextricable skein of the Clinton Foundation reached Ukrainian oligarch Victor Pinchuk, who had negotiated with Iran, which was a violation of the sanctions imposed by the United States on the Islamic Republic, according to *Newsweek* in April 2015. At the start of that year Pinchuk was confirmed as the greatest individual contributor to the Clinton Foundation with at least $8.6 million. The oligarch is the fourth wealthiest person in Ukraine owning the Interpipe Group, manufacturer of oil and gas pipelines, which according to *Newsweek* exported supplies to Iran during the years 2011 and 2012, including railroad parts and everyday products used in the oil and gas sectors. Due to all of this, Interpipe could have violated the sanctions imposed on Iran while it was very obsequious to the Clinton couple.

In May 2013 the book *Clinton Cash* was published in the U.S. by writer Peter Schweizer, which pointed out new accusatory elements against the dubious practices of the Clinton couple. Throughout its 245 pages the book highlights that since leaving the White House in 2001, the Clintons have participated in a series of suspect relationships with shady characters from various parts of the world, amassing more than a $130 million fortune in exchange for favors.

The economic contacts of the family which the work highlights spread to countries such as Colombia or Haiti, India or Congo, a wide geography where the couple has on repeated occasions muddled the lines between a private enterprise, public service, philanthropy and friendship, exposing themselves to conflicts of interest, according to the book.

Frank Giustra, a mining sector magnate in Canada, would have used his relations with the Clinton Foundation since the year 2005 to do business in different parts of the world, including Colombia, Mexico, Brazil and Haiti.

"What couple in U.S. politics would be so bold as to have one of the two accepting money from foreign businesses and governments, while the other is directing the foreign policy of the United States?" asks Schweizer.

Much ahead of the date of publication of the book, the powerful Clinton machinery launched a bombardment of the news media mobilizing the organisms in control of the liberal media denouncing the book as a hack.

In an article appearing in the *New York Post*, a month after the publication of the book, Schweizer declares that Hillary's claim to not know about the transfer of uranium —the material used to build nuclear weapons—to Vladimir Putin from the United States, while she was Secretary of State, goes beyond being an admission of extreme executive negligence about a National Security topic, becoming a dangerous act of corruption because "in the first place it caused those investors that benefited from the supply of uranium to donate collectively $145 million to the Clinton Foundation". And the author adds: "Does she honestly expect that Americans will believe that she simply didn't know about the agreement that was under consideration at her own State Department?"

On the other hand, Mary Anastasia O'Grady was writing in *The Wall Street Journal*, in March 2015, that the Clinton Foundation has in its donor list Brazilian construction company OAS and the Interamerican Development Bank, BID, which have given it between $1 and $5 million.

"OAS has been involved in the news because it is involved in the corruption scandal of the state oil company Petrobras. In November the Brazilian police arrested three high executives of the OAS due to their supposed role in a case of bribery and inflated contracts. The donation that OAS made to the Clinton Foundation is worth looking at because of the power that Bill Clinton has in Haiti, where the construction company has received contracts from the IDB".

Development banks are subject to ridicule by economists because while the banks proclaim that they fight against poverty they are particularly good at building empires. The same could be said about the Clintons in Haiti. A few months after Hillary became Secretary of State in 2009, Bill was designated as a special envoy to the UN in Haiti. This provided the Clintons great decision-making power in assigning American foreign aid to the small country. After the 2010 earthquake, they gathered even greater influence with the designation of Bill as co-president of the Interim Haiti Recovery Commission. The State Department began to direct those interested in competing for contracts in the country to the Clinton Foundation. "To be on good terms with Bill is important to anyone wanting to benefit from U.S. aid headed to Haiti" was the point made by this American columnist.

O'Grady adds that perhaps it will be easier to understand IDB donations as the State Department plays a key role in the approval of financing for this bank in the U.S. "The IDB told me in an email that in 2014 it made a donation to the Clinton Foundation of $150,000 for the Future of the Americas meeting. Between 2009 and 2013 it donated another $925,000 to finance expenses and activities for the planning and design of seven forums on public policy… in which relevant leaders on key issues to the work of the bank would be able to exchange ideas, strengthen their understanding and forge new and stronger alliances."

The problem with the Clintons in Haiti, concludes O'Grady, is that regardless of where you go "they are there with an appearance of a conflict of interests. It is not very likely that Haiti will win the long struggle against corruption when the U.S. government guarantees a former president wide power, with little supervision for him to distribute hundreds of millions of dollars amid so much misery."

On the other hand, the Clinton email scandal while she was in charge of the Department of State, between 2009 and 2013, takes on a specially delicate character because in that period took place the terrorist attack against the U.S. consulate in Benghazi, on September 11, 2012, which had as a balance the assassination of four U.S. diplomats, including Ambassador Chris Stevens, focusing attention on the U.S. Secretary of State for her unwise handling of the crisis in the region. Clinton was criticized above all for her initial manipulations which attributed the attack to an angry mob which was protesting a video which made fun of the prophet Mohammed, Later on the primary presidential candidate was forced to rectify the claim and the Obama Administration tried to rest importance from the Benghazi attack, as it behooved it since the presidential elections where approaching in November 2012, in which the president was seeking reelection. Hillary is such a friend of the poor that, acting as sensitive to the poor, she visited on April 7, 2016 the New York City subway and had a problem which was captured by television cameras. The presidential primary candidate was trying to pose as a common-man type, close to the people and their problems, and so she went down to the subway turnstile, but her lack of practice in using the metro card got her in trouble, a typical issue for those not in the habit of using the train, and she was unable to pass the card correctly to gain passage. Only with the aid of her stunned advisors, and after five unsuccessful attempts, the candidate was finally able to gain access to the platform to board a Metro train to The Bronx. So, the Metro role playing, or trying to look sensitive to the poor, no matter how much she ties doesn't go over well for this multimillionaire.

Ted Cruz

From the multimillionaire, white, Democrat and senior citizen we shall briefly take a look at a young, almost poor Republican primary candidate of Hispanic origin, or more precisely, of Cuban origin, named Ted Cruz. The first thing that stands out is that the press, so given to auscultate even the tonsils when Republicans or real conservative Republicans are involved, has not found up to now any skeletons, or at least any significant skeletons in his closet.

The second thing that stands out is that Jimmy Carter, probably the worst president in the United States, 1977-1981, only to be outdone by Obama (according to the prestigious consulting company Gallup, in an opinion report, only 43% of Americans approve of Obama's administration, curiously just a year before he opted for reelection, against 51% which Carter had reached in the same period but in 1980, when he lost to Ronald Reagan, who, before his reelection had a 54) has confessed that he would prefer magnate Donald Trump rather than ultra-conservative Ted Cruz in the White House, and additionally considers that Hillary will end up being the candidate of the Democratic Party. "I believe that I would elect Trump, which will surprise many of you. The reason is that Trump has already demonstrated to be completely malleable. I don't think he has any fixed posture for which to fight for in the White House", said Carter, according to what was published in his local newspaper *The Atlanta Journal-Constitution*.

"Cruz is not malleable. He defends positions situated well to the right which he would defend in the White House," added Carter in March 2016 during a press conference in the British Parliament.

"Trump is completely malleable (his ideas are flexible, changing)", added Carter. "I do not believe that he has very fixed or inflexible postures. In comparison, Ted Cruz is not at all malleable. His ideas are of the extreme right, in my opinion, and he would implement them inflexibly if he were to become president", he concluded. Carter didn't refer to Marco Rubio or to John Kasich, the other two Republican primary candidates in the campaign at the time. Okay, without trying to favor one or the other, but if there were no other available argument, Carter's reasoning would be sufficient to make a sensible voter decide for Cruz against Trump. It would suffice for our hypothetical elector to simply turn around Carter's opinion regarding the adjective in question: not malleable positive, malleable negative. The truth is that only a man with a decent sense of society, or with a counter-nature reality, could define a malleable personality as more positive than a non malleable. Simply go to *Webster's Dictionary* to see the various meanings of the adjective malleable:

- (of a metal or other material) able to be hammered or pressed permanently out of shape without breaking or cracking.
- Synonyms: pliable, ductile, plastic, pliant, soft, workable "a malleable substance" easily influenced, "Anna was shaken enough to be malleable."

In English, *malleable* is perhaps a more negative adjective: *An example of malleable is a person whose decisions are constantly influenced by her peers' opinions, Know Your Dictionary* (Love to Know Corp.)

Can you imagine what it would mean for the U.S. and for the Western World to have a president whose decisions are constantly influenced by the opinions of his colleagues, or even worse, by polls or the ups and downs of public opinion or everyday politicking? I am not sure that Trump is malleable, it is only Carter's opinion, and that he would prefer him because of it, for being malleable. The truth is that, given the dangers of the present, what the world needs the least is a malleable in the Oval Office.

Cruz has been labeled anti-immigrant, when in fact he has been a declared defender of immigration reform which would strengthen the border and which would encourage legal immigration, that is, opposed to the immigration measures decreed by Obama, nicknamed Deporter-in-Chief, who wants at all cost, even at the cost of what is constitutional, to leave a historic legacy on everything he touches. Thus, if King Midas would turn everything into gold, Obama turns it into history.

On numerous occasions Senator Cruz has criticized Obama's measures regarding immigration reform, which he argues would have meant amnesty for 11 million illegal immigrants who live in the country and a reward to those that violated, at time for worthy reasons one must say, the national borders.

The Senator has declared that in order to attract the Hispanic vote he would highlight the values of faith, family, country and hard work which he shares with that community. Subversive and Fascist values to the delicate ears of the progressives of the country.

Cruz accuses Democrats and Obama of treating immigration as a partisan issue and of trying to scare the Hispanic community to vote in a monolithic way for his party. In his opinion, for Congress to approve immigration reform it is necessary to reach an agreement regarding two priorities: close off the border and encourage legal immigration, not the illegal one. "I am the son of a legal immigrant and I am a great sympathizer of legal immigration" Cruz emphasized to the press in April 2015, facing those that were accusing him of being anti-immigrant, and referring to his Cuban origins. "To facilitate the path to citizenship for those that are here illegally is unfair to those who reside here legally" and to those that are trying to do it respecting the law" the Republican Senator emphasized.

But Cruz would not only eliminate Obama's executive orders in relation to the immigration issue, but he has also committed to eliminating all executive orders by the President "on his first day in the government". This would obviously imply the reversal of all the process of reestablishing relations with the Cuban dictatorship of General Raúl Castro and the lifting of sanctions against the regime of Iran, both supported by the decrees that the Democrat President loves so much.

Another point in favor of the not malleable Ted is that he stands out as one of the primary candidates who has opposed, from the start, the Affordable Care Act known as Obamacare, and he opposes it so much that three years ago he conducted a filibuster in the well of the Senate to manifest his opposition to this reform by reading from the children's book *Green Eggs and Ham,* written by Theodor Seuss Geisel, to the disgust of Democrats and woe to those that usually deny the artistic and literary sensibility of those not malleable men of the right, because even sensibility is denied to those that defiantly are opposed to enter through the straight and narrow sphincter of the times, that is, to follow politically correct guidelines, enlightened fanatical dogmas, of a society in downward spiral in the Post-Modernity of each day.

Obamacare has shown to be a failure bringing about more problems than the ones it was supposedly trying to solve, not only in the health field but also in the economy as a whole, which was sustained from the start upon falsehoods and without bipartisan support. Obama knowingly lied on various public appearances stating that the health law would allow people to keep their doctors and insurance and would in fact lower their costs. And so, when the health bill, a 2,700-page document which Congresspersons were not allowed to read—a superfluous prohibition in fact, because if there had been a Congressperson willing to stoically read this undecipherable document, he would still, at the time of this second edition, be reading it trying to understand what in heaven's name it says. But Nancy Pelosi, Speaker of the House of Representatives at that time, demanded that legislators vote on the health law and then to read it later, mimicking the Socialist and moderate practice of shooting first and asking later, as they enjoy immunity.

Cruz, the nonmalleable, and still up to now, non-spoiled, to the horror of progressives who are not the poor of this world, denies the novel of global warming —the last snowfalls apparently support him—is opposed to homosexual marriage, favors the death penalty and favors a U.S. foreign policy which doesn't give up its status as the first economic and military power in a world threatened at every turn by militant Islamism, empowered mainly by religious and cultural relativism, the malleability, in fact, of a West which, confusing the symbol with the actual concept being symbolized, manifests itself thusly with a decree, similar to a mantra, that it is the same God as a horse; a world marked by the Imperial appetite of powers such as Russia, China and Iran, and by the sputum of North Korea; all of which is augmented in recent times by the erroneous foreign policy of the U.S.

The Donald Trump Phenomenon

WE HAD POINTED OUT before that Donald Trump is not properly a Republican. The essential difference between Trump and Cruz is that the former seems basically to be a populist, closer to the late Venezuelan leader Hugo Chávez than to a typical American politician, a comparison which also fits President Obama.

Trump had never before registered as a Republican while contributing large amounts of money to the campaigns of Democrats. Thus, in August 2015 this very same magnate said during a televised debate in the Republican primary campaign that Democrat Hillary Clinton attended his wedding because he had donated money to her foundation.

"I told Hillary Clinton to come to my wedding and she came to my wedding. I had donated to her foundation" explained Trump, who used this example, in which he was the protagonist, to prove that "the system is rigged" "I gave to a foundation which supposedly was going to do good. I didn't know that it would go to pay for private airplanes throughout the world" the real estate mogul added. "I was a businessman. I donated to everybody. When they called me I donated. And you know what? When I needed something from them, two or three years later, I would call them and there they were for me" he acknowledged.

The candidate responded in this fashion to the questions of the debate moderators, who were questioning him about his past donations to both Hillary and her family foundation. But in 2012 he had called Clinton, in Fox News, a fantastic woman. "I am partial, because I've known her for a long time. I live in New York. She lives in New York. Really I get along with her and her husband as well". What is undeniable here is that the billionaire did his financing in Manhattan, that Clinton was the Senator from the State of New York, and that both moved in the same exclusive conclaves that mix happily, eclectically and pragmatically fortune, fame and politics in the society of fashion runways. Donald donated to the campaign of Hillary for Senate and she was invited to the third wedding of the magnate in Palm Beach, Florida in January 2005. But now, in the electoral scrimmage the billionaire has called the multimillionaire in Fox News as "the worst State Secretary in the history of the United States." She, for her part, has labeled him a "racist" and a "misogynist" while at the same time accusing him of dividing the country, as if Obama were not the great divider of the country with his class struggle and his historicism, and as if she had not been a preponderant part of his government. Trump donated $4,100 to the Hillary for Senate campaign, according to the website Politifact, and gave more than $100,000 to the Clinton Foundation. However, presently Hillary says that no, they are not friends at all, that at most they were acquaintances, and rather removed. Yet the media has documented that their daughters, Ivanka Trump and Chelsea Clinton are close friends who have vacationed together with their respective husbands.

And so Trump would not be a Republican by tradition nor by thought, or by principle, and doesn't fit in as a true conservative. Cruz, in turn, is motivated by philosophy and sustained by a solid intellectual foundation, a cum laude graduate at Princeton University, with a bachelor's degree from the Woodrow Wilson School in 1992, magna cum laude from Harvard's School of Law with a Juris Doctor degree in 1995, where he was selected to be Executive Editor of the Harvard Law Review and founding Editor of the Harvard Latino Law Review, endowed with a strong constitutionalism, and by the same token, a conservatism permeated by a strong libertarian influence and of a foundational individualism strictly American. Ted was the first Texas Attorney General of Hispanic origin and also became the youngest person to ever occupy that position in the United States.

Despite the media propaganda that usually accuses Cruz of being anti-Hispanic, in fact it was the Hispanic vote, to the tune of 32%, according to a poll conducted by Edison Research, which was fundamental in garnishing his victory in the Texas primary, where he obtained 99 delegates while Trump got 38.

"Part of the explanation lies in the fact that Ted Cruz is the son of a pastor," said in December to the BBC World Carol Swain, professor at Vanderbilt University, anticipating good results for the Cuban American Senator in Texas. "Voters know that Cruz was brought up as a Christian. Among the most conservative Christians, shared principles of faith are more important than other considerations such as race, social class or ethnicity. It is not surprising that he is popular with this group and I believe that he has gained credibility through his father and through his own expressions of faith," Swain states.

Even through the eyes of this conservative electorate, Cruz could have benefited from being the son of a Cuban who abandoned the island due to the regime of Fidel Castro, keeping in mind the strong anti-Communist tradition of American Evangelicals, according to Paul Harvey in the same publication, a political scientist at the University of Colorado. Harvey also points out that the Evangelical faith is growing among Hispanic in the country. "Evangelicals know that, to a certain point, the future of their movement is there" adds the academic.

And thus, in my previous book *Mitos del antiexilio* (Miami, in Spanish, 2007; Miami, in English, 2007; Milan, 2008), we demonstrate how the Cuban exile is an offspring of the leftist-leaning Cuban republic prior to 1959 (Fidel Castro didn't come out of thin air but was rather a product of it). Except in particular niches within the new generations of Cuban Americans, we cannot properly describe a true right, we would have to say that Cruz and Rubio are examples of exceptions of authentic right among island exiles, or better still, of their descendants.

Trump and the Hinge Time

AND TO FINISH, WE cannot but mention some considerations regarding Trump and the epochal milieu that has yielded him. It is unquestionable, to the keen observer, that large sectors of American society, beyond party affiliation or ideology, and especially among people that sweat for a living, feel desperate on account of the misbegotten political solutions that the Obama Administration has made, and that therefore, they don't see a way out by way of the traditional political machineries or methodologies. Therefore, the seismic movements that we feel on the surface of American society are not anything other than manifestations of ferocious fractures and radical telluric readjustments in the deepest layers, in the abysm of the social subsoil, there, where the monsters of the mythical night emerge, wait and live; before history. Those physical formations, expressions of the spiritual plane, of the social subconscious, to use a rationalistic term, no longer believe in the customary usage. They are in search of a different leader, a messiah if it be, who could equally be an enlightened one as a demagogue, someone who will say, sincerely or not, but that will say, what they are feeling and they don't know how or can't say. This is an exceptional historical period, a crucial time, a time for the selected ones, as many other times in the past of humankind, but those tremendous times, which escape all the "should be", that escape all rationality, morality, humanism, conceptualizations of good and evil, notions of greatness or baseness, convenience or pragmatism, are as likely to give birth to a Caesar as to a Caligula, a Christ as likely as a Mohammed, a Churchill instead of a Hitler; a Saint as opposed to a Satan. We don't know why one versus the other, of the mythical mechanisms that determine them, later will come the explanations and theorizations, more or less misbegotten, more or less on the mark, but always about consummated events, over the consequences, not about the causes, about the physical and superficial, not about what is deep and spiritual; at the end, a schema mounted over appreciations and prejudices, childishness and perversions, delusions and disagreements, furies, and frustrations, idealizations and idiocies of the scribes, historians, academics and later academics.

We embrace a change of era, of paradigm in all human orders, what was will no longer be, what up to yesterday we understood to be certain will now appear to us doubtful, or false of all falsity, what we accepted as good and intelligent will appear to us evil and ignorant, what convenient, inconvenient, and this will be seen not only in politics, in thought, in society and in customs but also, if they survive, in the expressions of art and literature; there will be a return to the roots, all that dilates contracts, what goes returns, what goes down up, what dies lives, this, for the cycles of the cycles, amen. To be modern, as we already pointed out, according to Kundera, we will have no other option than being anti-modern. With art and literature it will happen that from the puerile, intimate, convoluted, banal, anatomical, sometimes anal, of the last era, they will return to their primordial sources in which they were manifestations of the spirit, sacred in themselves, determinants upon the world of phenomena; there will be a return to pictorial images as tools of operational magic or to its sublimations of religious scenes, first, or of the great battles, landscapes and historical personalities later; to the metaphors of foundational poems and mythological narratives first, and to epic poems and epic poems later, not literally perhaps, which should not be exaggerated either, but there will undoubtedly be a return to the poetics and novelistics of the past, to the traditional forms that correspond to the authentic contents of a sacred mandate behind the works, the authors who will do those works, a mandate from the unconscious, we would say, to explain more or less rationally something that is not rational, but allows a better understanding of what we say.

All of this will happen or art, literature, thought and politics, society and government structures will disappear, at least as they have existed in the West up to now and for many centuries.

We are again at the point of nationalisms, now people don't declare themselves citizens of the world in the globalist and postmodern vulgarization of the famous phrases by Socrates: "I am a citizen not of Athens or of Greece, but rather of the world." More or less it is said or considered a citizen not of a country but rather of a region, not of a region but rather of a city, as men considered themselves many centuries ago at the time of Socrates, who was a modern man and pronounced the famous phrase in the context of the anti-modernity of the common people of his time, as they considered themselves citizens of a city. Something that was too restrictive for the wise man. Well, Greek wise man, considered to be one of the great, both in Western philosophy as in world philosophy, he now intersects with the moderns of our day, who begin to stop being so given the unsuspected turns of reality, obstinate and counterrevolutionary, which makes the people of the 21st century declared themselves citizens of Paris, Madrid, Miami, Milan, New York, Buenos Aires or Berlin.

But not only that, in extreme cases the people declare their belonging and territorial fidelity not to a city but to a neighborhood, if not to a city block, and perhaps not to a block at all but to a bar on that block, a citizen of that bar, they declare themselves boastfully demanding a beer.

Thus, not only do nationalisms increase but, paradoxically, this coincides in some regions of the planet with the disappearance of national states, with a fragmentation into groups linked to specific, ethnic, religious, political, and even sexual interests that they would in some measure be assimilated to the hordes and tribes of the past; in fact, the disparate urban tribes have long been spoken of among young people united by the most insignificant identities, determined by the neighborhoods in which they live, the symbols they have tattooed, the music they hear, the fashion they follow, the hairstyle they wear or the way they assume the sexual act.

The horde precedes the clan, the clan the tribe, the tribe the cities states, the cities states the kingdoms, and the kingdoms the empire or imperial idea. It is more or less what happened in antiquity. But at present, along with the fragmentation mentioned, the imperial drive persists. This is what we see in Putin's Russia, Xi Jinping's China, or, in his degraded way, in Raúl's and Fidel Castro's Cuba. The imperial idea is more concrete, and is macabre, with ISIS or Islamic State of Iraq and al-Sham, also known as the Islamic State of Iraq and the Levant, which covers a large transnational region including Israel, Lebanon and Syria. That which is now known as the Islamic State, began as Al-Qaeda in Afghanistan, and later in Iraq, now able to be assimilated by the hordes or tribes of the past, but not less dangerous because we should not forget that it was the organization behind Bin Laden and the terrorist attacks that toppled the Twin Towers of New York in 2001, which is now embodied in a strong will to strengthen, expand and occupy. Thus, if Al-Qaeda in its stage of horde or tribe was only interested in attacking and damaging, ISIS, in its imperial stage, is also interested in occupying and controlling territories, so that they already dominate in the old-fashioned part of Iraq and Syria, in what they call a caliphate. So ISIS or Islamic State would be all of a terrorist group, a horde, a tribe, a de facto state and an imperial spasm.

Caliphate comes from *khalifa,* which would mean successor, Muhammad's successor, the founder of Islam. The caliphate of the original successor occupied the Middle East, North Africa and the Iberian Peninsula between 622 and 750. Throughout history there were five other recognized caliphates and the last of them was that of the Ottoman Empire, which disappeared in 1923 when the Republic of Turkey was founded. ISIS wants to revive that empire of the past. In light of this, the U.S. may need to retake, if it ever desisted from it, the old imperial idea.

It is possible that the world, in the face of fragmentation, returns to empires. Let us not forget that in the past empires came to impose peace, order, prosperity and freedom in vast regions of the planet dominated by chaos, desolation, misery and death (a consequence especially of the continuous wars and battles among multiple tribes), and who, at the point of the sword, were a decisive civilizing factor. Let us not forget also that the national states are an artificial creation of the modern world, which emerged only in the middle of the 17th century, through the Treaty of Westphalia in 1648, after the Thirty Years' War, fought in Central Europe, mainly in the Holy Roman Empire (Germanic), that is consolidated in the 19th century, after the Industrial Revolution, the American Revolution and the French Revolution. Thus the national state would, to a certain extent, be the result both of rationalist pragmatism and of revolutionary romanticism.

Contrary to what we have been told, the disintegration of the Spanish Empire, after the loss of incalculable human lives, devastation and economic ruin during the long and multiple wars for South American independence, and the establishment of subsequent republics, which in turn gave rise to another endless series of wars, revolutions, warlords and dictatorships, probably signified the greatest human disaster in this hemisphere which, even today, suffers the aftermath.

So that at present we could be in a time hinge, one in which the Spirit of the Times becomes another. Thus we will see those modes and systems which seemed to us imperishable, even impeccable, to collapse like butter-chests in the midday sun, and to the luminaries within those modes and systems, movie stars and spectators, writers, intellectuals, businessmen, journalists , politicians, pontiffs, officials, messiahs of climate change and other trivialities, dwarf and disappear in the same nothing that they always were, because the epochal muse that supported them, swelled and oversized it will have disappeared previously, to give way to the Spirit of another era which will bring with it other demands and despair, problems and congratulations, dangers and powers, priorities and expectations, sins and privations, agonies and abundances, vices and virtues that will require another kind of hero in the spheres of human action, especially in the spheres of art, letters, religion, politics and war; because war will have ended the false sense of security of the modern world as a known place, domestic or domesticated, disengaged from the divine, from the mysteries of existential cycles, which come, with good fortune, to fatten the ego and to legislate later on those desires and perversions, where liberties and sustenance are given by deeds, where death, disease, old age and misery are eliminated by decree; thus we see marathons or months dedicated to the fight against cancer, muscular atrophy, autism, the arms race, hunger, frigidity or gender violence; a world to walk beautiful, healthy, muscular and warm, with all the holes satisfied, and where the mere fact of disconnecting from the Internet terrifies us.

In the first edition of this book, in 2011, we had said that the Democratic Party was bifurcating towards the margins, cracking the social body, Latin Americanizing itself in short, but today that would be a fact not only in that political machine, but also in its counterpart, the Republican Party, and beyond these machineries, in the whole of American society. Trump is not the cause of anything, neither is Obama, both the consequence of a long and scabrous process descending in the social, of disparagement and defamation of traditional values by means of the media, the school system, universities, showbiz celebrities, and opinion leaders, but this, in turn, is not the cause of anything, but the consequence of a profound phenomenon that nests in our thoughts, but rather in the psyche and in the human soul, so that all things and phenomena of this world are given and would operate according to the prediction that everything manifested has its cause in something deeper, previous and not manifested.In the essay *Del fanatismo religioso al fanatismo racionalista* (From religious fanaticism to rationalistic fanaticism) (journal *Otro Lunes,* #34), we sought to deepen in the descent or degradation of Modernity, or Post-Modernity, as they call it, to find out that there was a type of society determined by the actual regimentation of ancient or traditional civilizations in their subordination to the powers of the sacred rather than to the powers of this world and where, obviously, the powers of this world perceived as disengaged or deserted from the powers of the sacred run the risk of falling down headless. Societies, prior to the Renaissance and the Reformation, which would be organized vertically from the high monarch to the lowly serfs and other members of the masses that formed the base of the pyramid, going first through the feudal nobility, the clergy, the various religious orders, the orders of chivalry, guilds, lodges and tradesmen and other professions that, in some cases, would later evolve into speculative masonry, the same Freemasonry that would play a decisive role during the advent of modern society with the crucible of historical phenomena like the American Revolution, the Enlightenment and the French Revolution. It is proper to make a distinction between the Masonic lodges that influence the unleashing of events in France from those in North America, between the thinkers of the French Enlightenment and those of the English Enlightenment (most of whom would also be Freemasons), and, obviously, between the civil societies that spawned both phenomena. Let us say that the difference would be, fundamentally, that civil societies in the Anglo-American sphere would be freer and more stable than societies in the Frankish sphere. Perhaps this is because freedom and stability depend to a large extent on the upward or downward direction of societies.

Thus the Italian baron and traditionalist philosopher Julius Evola, who has perhaps delved the most into the analysis of modernity, asserts that the true cause of the decline of political ideas in the contemporary

West lies precisely in the fact that the spiritual values which once impregnated the social order have come to mean less, with nothing to replace them.

The problem is, says Evola, that we have descended to the level of economic, industrial, military, administrative or even sentimental considerations and factors, without realizing that all this is nothing more than mere matter, necessary perhaps but never sufficient to produce a solid and rational social order, self-supporting, in the same way that the simple encounter of mechanical forces will never produce a living being.

So the United States was founded not so much as a democracy but more as a constitutional republic, but was founded above all looking upward, as would be shown by the fact that the Masonic lodges of the thirteen colonies, New Hampshire, Massachusetts, Rhode Island, Connecticut, New York, New Jersey, Pennsylvania, Delaware, Maryland, Virginia, North Carolina, South Carolina and Georgia were the definitive focus of the insurrection against British rule.

So important for American history would Freemasonry be (according to the National Heritage Museum and documentation in general of this organization) that most of those who signed the Declaration of Independence of the United States, on July 4, 1776, were distinguished sons of the Widow, as members of this fraternity were known, including: Ellery, Franklin, Hancock, Hewes, Hooper, Paine, Stockton, Walton and Whipple.

Nine of the thirteen delegates who signed the articles of the new confederation were Masons: Adams, Carroll, Dickinson, Ellery, Hancock, Harnett, Laurens, Roberdau and Bayard Smith, and Masons were also the men who signed the American Constitution: Bedford , Blair, Brearley, Broom, Carroll, Dayton, Dickinson, Franklin, Gilman, King, McHenry, Patterson and Washington. The great majority of the congressmen who ratified these agreements were also members of the Masonic brotherhood and, in addition, the great majority of the high command of the Colonial Army that faced the British troops was constituted by initiates in the mysteries under the aegis of the Square and Compass.

The fact is that speculative Freemasonry has exerted a determining influence on the establishment of the American nation, an influence that has been greater than that exerted by any other institution in the history of this country.

But it is not only a matter of Freemasonry in regard to American holy things, for it is not possible to forget that the Pilgrims who arrived on the Mayflower did so driven by religion and to escape religious persecution in the Old World.

Although it is good to note also that religiosity in itself would not suffice for the upward trend in a given society, but rather a certain doctrine of *dharma* through which the egalitarian concept of human nature is rejected, fundamentally driven by the Jewish heritage Christian and later taken up by Jesuits, Protestants and the Enlightenment.

A religiosity in short that substitutes the concept of *human nature* for a more qualified *own nature*, which each must develop for the fulfillment of individual freedom within society.

The descendant societies flee from the religious, but they do not escape from it, but they are based on another religiosity, going through celestial utopias to terrestrial utopias, materialistic utopias that reach their climax, bloody orgasm, with Socialism in its timely derivations, Nazism and Communism, two wings of the same ugly bird, black one, the other red, one nationalist, the other internationalist: apotheosis both of supra reason and supra modernity.

At a time when men, not satisfied with expelling Christ from the firmament of their tormented minds, expel all the gods that there have ever been, and then outdo themselves coming to repeat the Christ process, but vice versa because if Christ is God made man who lets himself be crucified, now they make gods of men, maximum leaders they call them, before whom they end up crucified.

Wow we have had to deal with Lenin, Stalin, Hitler, Castro, Chávez and the Maduros of this world! a transition from religious obscurantism to rationalist obscurantism, from divine dogmas to social dogmas; from Moses to Marx, from the Holy Office of the Inquisition to the Department of Revolutionary Guidance and State Security, a setback for truth. One in which modern Western society, disbelieving its foundational myths, tales of the adolescent age of humanity they call them, is allowed to dominate by dysfunctional myths. A society that wants to emancipate itself through individuation goes back to the amorphous mass of its tribal stages; to an archaic group think.

At the time of Marx and the abrupt and agitated political and economic liberalization of the 19th century, civil society, conceived as a material and concrete subject, acquired a supposed capacity for action and movement that would be nothing other than mortality and stagnation. And from the Marxist civil society we pass on to a Gramscian civil society, both unnatural. The Italian Antonio Gramsci merges in a single item the civil and the state and, like the Catholics in Aristotelian-Thomist version, but without the holy, bets for the perfect society, and thinks that when the State is everything, the civil society recovers with it its ideal concretion and consolidates its ethical, political and cultural hegemony.

Gramsci predicted that political power over society had to be taken from school and academic systems, cultural centers and the media. Contrary to Marxism, Gramscism has nothing of revolutionary workers, but a lot of revolutionary intellectualism. Just as what is happening now in the Western world, starting with the USA. And if the U. S. has embodied freedom for at least two centuries, it is probable that now, thanks to Gramscism that would begin to no longer be true.

So Obama and Trump would be more a result of Gramscism than of Marxism, not so Sanders, who by his advanced age would be mostly a Marxist result. But more than Trump, Obama would be nothing more than the final product of a Gramscian-style unnatural society. Trump would rather be the product of an equally materialist utopia, which would be that of easy, speculative, globalist financial capitalism, short-term and short-sighted, of quick wealth and without many moral or principled considerations, closer to the old merchant, in this case of worldwide reach at the touch of keyboard, than the true capitalist.

Under the Gramscian system democracy degenerates into demagoguery. But demagoguery becomes a dictatorship when politicians are obliged to satisfy at all costs, to reach power, the majorities dominated not by the mind, but by the stomach or the crotch.

Thus, in postmodernism, anti-system strategists have openly declared that a civil society would be the way to undermine bourgeois democracies, and so certain rights are supported, created or exacerbated, activism in favor of homosexuals, environmentalists, feminists, pacifists, marihuana, illegal immigration, relativist and multiculturalist. Thus it is legislated through the desire, the emotions, the prejudices and the sentimentality of each horde or social tribe, and a right is created for each appetite, without meaning, not any longer of a nation but without common sense.

The class struggle of Marxism has been replaced by the social fragmentation of Gramscism. And the Gramscian society requires, as in the world of Orwell, a neo language that perverts not the word but the thought, and not the thought but the reality. Thus, together with the world of George Orwell, that of the novel *1984*, and of Aldous Huxley, that of the novel *A Brave New World*, man becomes a happy slave, having forgotten the darkness of the soul, dazzled by the speed and luminescence of the screens on the virtual highways, on a journey to nothingness.

Both the Tea Party malcontents who followed Cruz, and the most heterogeneous and heterodox, grouped with Trump on the Republican side, and even disgruntled Sanders on the Democratic side, would be signs of the new times, that something smells a rotten in the

American social organism, and Western by extension. People have the real or imaginary sensation, which for that matter is the same, that there has been cheating and lying for some time, that nothing is as it seems, that what they sell us as good is bad, and that what they sell us as bad is good, that if in the past, as in Cuba and the old Communist countries, they began to shoot the press to impose the dictatorship, now it is the other way around: the press is the one that shoots, with virtuality and treachery, but it shoots, it kills with lies the unarmed masses, or manipulates them, disparages the rebels, the inconvenient disappears, and while it pretends to defend the poor it serves the powerful who appear to be the same thing; The Clintons and the Obamas would be the clearest example.

A macabre game of mirrors and trick cards, where the individual has all the freedoms of what is trivial yet increasingly less fundamental freedoms, an individual who paints his hair with colored flames and dresses and drives in a bizarre way to be different from the masses, as the media commercials tell him at all times, but increasingly becomes an element, an entity, a number, disregarded of all greatness, or looks of grandeur, a statistic that makes up the great brainless mass, acquiescent against the infinity of the screens that induce products, passions and emotions, that numb and distract from the soul (not surprisingly this season has been so successful for grisly television series of zombies).

And if Trump has declared that the system is broken, Senator Marco Rubio has just stated the same (April 14, 2016), noting that the U. S. Senate refused to discuss its proposal on reform of the Cuban Adjustment Act and of benefits to Cuban immigrants.

Senator Rubio was clearly displeased with this decision, and criticized the "political paralysis" that exists in Congress. "This is the reason why people are so tired of politics," said Rubio, who noted that until a month ago as a Republican presidential candidate he listened to voters about their frustrations with lawmakers. "You can vote for a Democrat, you can vote for a Republican, you can vote for a vegetarian. It doesn't matter who you vote for: Nothing happens. These people do nothing." "No one can discuss this," he added of his proposal, "and I cannot even get a vote on an amendment to change this."

And why not? According to Rubio, because his Republican colleagues say to him: "We cannot vote for the proposal because, if we give you your amendment, then we must also give the other side its amendment" (referring to the Democrats side).

Trump says things that connect to people's unconscious, which few politicians dare say but many people want to hear. At least he says them, we do not know if he will do them, but for now he is unstoppable in his popularity. Trump has the advantage of speaking to the emotions, while Cruz, without being a rationalist, speaks more to reason and, we know, between emotions and reasons often emotions win out; even more in the primaries.

One thing seems to be clear: the candidate at the party convention in July who obtains the support of the required 1,237 delegates, must be the party's nominee or, if not, the one with the most delegates if we are to avoid what is known as a "negotiated convention". If Trump is the victor, the Republican National Committee must cope with it and refrain from maneuvers which, being perfectly legal, may not be ethical, to impose a candidate, be it Cruz or Kasich, or even a last-minute nominee, because it would fragment still more a fragmented party and, of course, would fragment an even more fragmented society, generating distrust, more than the existing one, in the electorate that will just feel cheated. Thomas E. Dewey was the last Republican candidate elected in a "negotiated convention", in 1948, soon to lose the elections against Democrat Harry S. Truman.

Trump told CNN's News Day program in March that a determination in that regard could end up generating violence and chaos, there would be riots, "I think bad things would happen." "I represent many millions of people ... If their rights are stolen, I think there would be problems like they have never been seen before," said the billionaire.

But not only Trump, Cruz said the same thing, on the same date, against a "negotiated convention" ensuring that it would be a real disaster. "There are some in Washington who have febrile dreams of a negotiated convention. They are unhappy with the way people are voting and they want to parachute in their favorite candidate, " Cruz told New Day.

"If it happens that we get to Cleveland and no one has 1,237 delegates, that Donald has a lot of delegates and that I have a lot of delegates and we are matched, then it's up to the delegates to decide." If this were not the case, "people would have every right to rebel," added the Texan senator.

A good point of agreement, a hint that the apparent opposites could complement, materialize in a single ballot to face a surely strengthened Hillary in the November presidential election.

The voters, or the forces behind the voters, will have the last word, and if any certainty we harbor over this campaign for the presidency is that the winner in November will determine, for many years, the downward drift or the ascending path of the American nation.

April 2016

EXODUS

This edition of *Cards in the mirror*
was held between Barcelona & Miami
in september
2020

© Photo by Delio Regueral

ARMANDO DE ARMAS WAS born on October 15, 1958 in Santa Clara, Cuba. He has a degree in Philology from the Central University of Las Villas. He was part of the human rights and independent culture movement within the island. He suffered persecution and arrests for his commitment to free writing. Imprisoned in 1989, he managed to escape from prison that same year. He left Cuba in 1994 in a spectacular escape under the persecution and fire from border guards, along with a group of friends, in a boat in the south of the island and in a journey of more than 600 miles to the Cayman Islands and of then on to Quintana Roo, Mexico. The magazine *Lettre International* of Berlin published, in German translation, a chronicle of his escape. In 1995, as part of a flotilla of exiles headed in protest to Havana, he survived the shipwreck of the *Sundown II* in the Florida Straits.

IIe has published the following books:

Mala jugada, (or Bad Play), stories, Miami, 1996, New York, 2012, written in Cuba and published in the United States. Stories from this book have been included in the anthology of Michi Straufeld, *Les Nouvelles de Cuba,* Metaillié Publishing House, Paris, and the anthology *Tales from Miami,* Polyhedron Publishing House, Barcelona, and the anthology *Kubánská* èítanka, Prague, by Margarita Mateová Palmerová and Stanislav Škoda. Also an account of this book was translated into German and published by the *Lettre International* magazine, Berlin.

Carga de la caballería (or Cavalry Charge) stories, Miami, 2006. The *Fingers* tale from this book was published by TheWriteDeal, New York, 2011. Moreover, this book of stories spent three weeks in the bestsellers list in Miami and was presented during the International Book Fair of that city in 2006.

Mitos del antiexilio, (or Myths of the Anti-Exile), essay, Miami, 2007, presented at several universities in the United States and the International Book Fair of Miami that year, two weeks on the bestsellers in that city. Published in English by the Alexandria Library Publishing House, 2007, and in Italian in 2008 by Editorial Spirali, presented with great media coverage at the Hotel Palace in Rome, and on subsequent tours in the cities of Milan, Senago, Bolognia and Florence. Among Spirali's best-selling books the year it was published.

Los naipes en el espejo, (or Cards in the Mirror) essay, NewYork, 2011.

La tabla, (or The Table) novel, Editorial Hispano Cubana, Madrid, 2008, presented that same year in Madrid, presented in 2009 at the Spanish Cultural Center of Miami, and invited to the International Book Fair of that city in November 2009. It was published after 18 years of being written in Cuba and smuggled out of the country and has been cataloged by some critics and scholars of the island literature as the "novel of the Cuban revolution."

Caballeros en el tiempo, (or Knights in Time), novel, Atmósfera Literaria Publishers, Madrid, 2013. Presented in Spain and the United States. This book could never be published in Cuba and was part of the protest literature inside the island, until it was smuggled out of the country by the author.

De Armas was selected to integrate the anthology of essays *La democrazia*, Milan, 2009, published by the

Università Internazionale del Secondo Rinascimento and the Editorial Spirali, which included intellectuals and thinkers from East and West.

Also appearing the book were interviews and valuations about life and the work of writers, *Scrittori, artisti,* Spirali, 2009, by writer and academician Armando Verdiglione (*Scrittori, artisti, in un'accezione nuova: nel secondo rinascimento l'oralità è il modo di scrittura dell'esperienza originaria. L'intreccio di queste conversazioni al di fuori degli schemi contribuisce al processo di valorizzazione della memoria: testimonianze, racconti, aneddoti, apologhi, paradigmi di vita, amicizia, battaglie intellettuali*)

De Armas has written articles, essays and testimonies for the magazine *Lettre Internacional,* Berlin, some as cover stories. As an author he has been interviewed by numerous European media, among them channel Art of French-German television, the television of Castille-La Mancha, Spain, *Corriere della Sera* and *Vanity Fair,* Italy. As well in the book *Cuba: Mémoires d´un Naugragueha,* Paris, 2009, published recently in Spanish under the title *El libro negro del castrismo,* by writer Jacobo Machover, which includes the testimony of intellectuals and personalities who suffered prison and persecution in Cuba.

In 2010 it was published in Spain the book, *Última novela: Cuba,* by scholar Ramón Luque from Universidad Rey Juan Carlos de Madrid, which is a study dedicated to the life and work of four Cuban exile writers, among them Armando de Armas.

Additionally, he was Vice-President of the PEN CLUB of Cuban Writers in Exile (London International PEN Chapter). On August 31, 2007, he was part of a delegation of Cuban exile leaders and legislators from the United States Congress who, invited by the Government of Poland, signed with Polish President Lech Kaczyński the Agreement for Democracy in Cuba , in the city of Lubin.

A well-known Hispanic media personality in the U.S., he participates as a weekly guest on highly rated television shows in South Florida. He also frequently participates as a guest on radio programs and serves as a weekly columnist in several media outlets.